The Naval Africa Expedition of World War I: The History and Legacy of the Battle for Lake Tanganyika in the African Interior

By Charles River Editors

The *Graf von Götzen*

About Charles River Editors

Charles River Editors is a boutique digital publishing company, specializing in bringing history back to life with educational and engaging books on a wide range of topics. Keep up to date with our new and free offerings with this 5 second sign up on our weekly mailing list, and visit Our Kindle Author Page to see other recently published Kindle titles.

We make these books for you and always want to know our readers' opinions, so we encourage you to leave reviews and look forward to publishing new and exciting titles each week.

Introduction

A modern picture of Lake Tanganyika

The Naval Africa Expedition of World War I

"It is both the duty and the tradition of the Royal Navy to engage the enemy wherever there is water to float a ship." – Admiral Sir Henry Jackson

World War I, also known in its time as the "Great War" or the "War to End all Wars", was an unprecedented holocaust in terms of its sheer scale. Fought by men who hailed from all corners of the globe, it saw millions of soldiers do battle in brutal assaults of attrition which dragged on for months with little to no respite. Tens of millions of artillery shells and untold hundreds of millions of rifle and machine gun bullets were fired in a conflict that demonstrated man's capacity to kill each other on a heretofore unprecedented scale, and as always, such a war brought about technological innovation at a rate that made the boom of the Industrial Revolution seem stagnant. World War I was the first truly industrial war, and it created a paradigm which reached its zenith with World War II and towards which virtually all equipment, innovation and training were dedicated throughout the Cold War and the remainder of the 20th century. To this day, modern warfare remains synonymous with tanks and mass infantry battles, although a confrontation of this nature has not occurred (except briefly during Operation Desert Storm) since World War II.

The enduring image of World War I is of men stuck in muddy trenches, and of vast armies deadlocked in a fight neither could win. It was a war of barbed wire, poison gas, and horrific losses as officers led their troops on mass charges across No Man's Land and into a hail of bullets. While these impressions are all too true, they hide the fact that trench warfare was dynamic and constantly evolving throughout the war as all armies struggled to find a way to break through the opposing lines.

This was the experience of most frontline soldiers during that great conflict, but it was not the only experience. In reality, World War I was fought in far more places, some thousands of miles away from France, including in Africa. The modern history of Africa was, until very recently, written on behalf of the indigenous races by white men, who had forcefully entered the continent during a particularly hubristic and dynamic phase of European history. In 1884, Prince Otto von Bismark, the German chancellor, brought the plenipotentiaries of all major powers of Europe together to deal with Africa's colonization in such a manner as to avoid provocation of war. This event - known as the Berlin Conference of 1884-1885 - galvanized a phenomenon that came to be known as the Scramble for Africa. The conference established two fundamental rules for European seizure of Africa. The first of these was that no recognition of annexation would granted without evidence of a practical occupation, and the second, that a practical occupation would be deemed unlawful without a formal appeal for protection made on behalf of a territory by its leader, a plea that must be committed to paper in the form of a legal treaty.

This began a rush, spearheaded mainly by European commercial interests in the form of Chartered Companies, to penetrate the African interior and woo its leadership with guns, trinkets and alcohol, and having thus obtained their marks or seals upon spurious treaties, begin establishing boundaries of future European African colonies. The ease with which this was achieved was due to the fact that, at that point, traditional African leadership was disunited, and the people had just staggered back from centuries of concussion inflicted by the slave trade. Thus, to usurp authority, to intimidate an already broken society, and to play one leader against the other was a diplomatic task so childishly simple, the matter was wrapped up, for the most part, in less than a decade. However, it would also set the stage for one of the oft-forgotten campaigns of World War I, and the aftermath of that campaign would affect the African continent for the next 100 years.

The Naval Africa Expedition of World War I: The History and Legacy of the Battle for Lake Tanganyika in the African Interior examines one of the most unique battles of World War I. Along with pictures of important people, places, and events, you will learn about the expedition like never before.

The Naval Africa Expedition of World War I: The History and Legacy of the Battle for Lake Tanganyika in the African Interior

About Charles River Editors

Introduction

   The Berlin Conference

   The Start of the War

   A Bold Scheme

   Mimi and *Toutou*

   The Naval Africa Expedition

   A Magnificent Journey

   The Battle for Lake Tanganyika

   Conclusion

   Online Resources

   Bibliography

Free Books by Charles River Editors

Discounted Books by Charles River Editors

The Berlin Conference

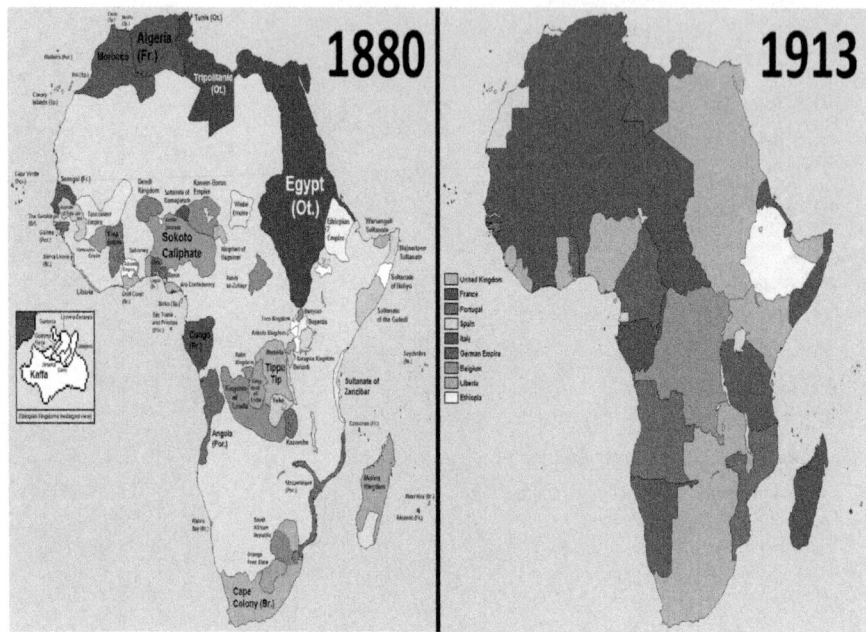

A map of African colonies in 1880 and 1913

"I do not want to miss a good chance of getting us a slice of this magnificent African cake." – Leopold II of Belgium

On the morning of Saturday, November 15, 1884, plenipotentiaries of all of the major powers of Europe gathered at the official residence of the German Reich Chancellor, Prince Otto von Bismarck. As each entered the yard, they were met at their carriage door by the Chancellor himself and then ushered into the library, where an informal reception took place. Then, as a body, they climbed the wide, ceremonial staircase to a second-floor reception room, where each took his allocated seat at a semi-circular table arranged before a large and detailed map of Africa pinned to the wall. Bismarck addressed the assembled delegates, outlining briefly the objectives of the meeting, after which, casting his eyes from left to right, he declared the Berlin Conference formally in session.

Bismarck

A depiction of Bismarck at the Berlin Conference

The Berlin Conference of 1884-85, a dry and rather formal affair, was nonetheless one of the most important and far-reaching gatherings of international power to take place at any time during the 19th century, and one that would deeply impact the course of European and African history up to the present day. In its simplest terms, the Berlin Conference sought to regulate the subdivision of Africa between the principal European powers in a manner that would not cause a major war between them. Only a somewhat desultory European interest had been shown in Africa to date, amounting to little more than a patchwork of competing spheres of influence. These were mostly private concerns — chartered companies displaying a national flag — but here and there, territories were being annexed and occupied, and in general, a rather unhealthy mood of competition was incubating over the question of Africa.

Perhaps the best example of this was the Witwatersrand, the gold-bearing region of the Transvaal Republic, nominally a British sphere of influence and certainly the most important theater of British capital adventure of the age. South Africa at that point was divided into four separate territories - two British colonies (Natal and Cape) and two independent Boer republics (Transvaal and Orange Free State) - and between these there existed enormous suspicion and antipathy. The superior weight of British capital and imperial reach allowed the British to dominate the Transvaal gold fields, but they did so very much to the chagrin of the Boer. The Boer were not by any means impoverished because of this, but as they prospered, they were ever vigilant toward any British threat against their sovereignty.

It was onto this rather tense economic and political stage that the Germans entered in 1884, annexing the territory of Damaraland, nominally the whole of modern-day Namibia, as a German colony. This immediately pitched the British into a fit of apprehension. What were German intentions? Was it the gold, the diamonds, the strategic ports, or all of the above? The British were acutely aware that the hatred felt toward them by the Boer could easily drive them into the arms of an opposing European power, and bearing in mind the ideological compatibility of Germany and Boer at that time, the Germans were in a position, should they choose, to wreak havoc on British interests in South Africa.

Then, perhaps, the signature event took place that set the tone for some sort of orchestration of competing interests in Africa. In 1877, Welsh American explorer Henry Morton Stanley emerged at the mouth of the Congo River, completing an expedition of 1,000 days to map the central lakes complex and explore the Congo River. Here was the definitive, Victorian template of African exploration. Stanley, known by the natives of the interior as *Bula Matari*, or the Breaker of Rocks, had left Zanzibar in 1874, traveling over land toward the continental divide, where his objective was to map the lakes of the Great Rift Valley, determine the source of the Nile, and explore the Lualaba River.

Stanley

Three years earlier, in 1871, Stanley made his name as an explorer through his successful search for Dr. David Livingstone. Livingstone had not been heard from in Africa since departing England in 1866, also in search of the source of the Nile, and the general assumption was that he was dead. Stanley at that time was a roving reporter for the *New York Herald*, and sensing a scoop, publisher James Gordon Bennett commissioned and funded an expedition, led by Stanley, to search the African interior to either locate Livingstone or confirm his death. On November 10, 1871, Stanley achieved precisely this, finding Livingstone impoverished and ill in the settlement of Ujiji, on the east shore of Lake Tanganyika, and greeting him, at least according to popular myth, with the now immortal words *"Doctor Livingstone, I presume."*

Livingstone

Despite his lamentable circumstances, Livingstone would not contemplate leaving. His work, he maintained, was here in Africa. But he shared with Stanley his conviction that a large river he had discovered, flowing northward through what would today be northern Zambia and southern Congo, and known as the Lualaba, was the mythical source of the River Nile. Stanley disagreed, suggesting that it was more likely to be the headwater of the Congo River, and it was to confirm this, and much else besides, that Stanley embarked on his second expedition in 1874.

And with his emergence at the mouth of the Congo River in 1877, his hair now white, he confirmed his theory, and he was hailed in all the usual places as the greatest explorer of the age. Stanley, however, while hardly shunning the publicity, had in mind much more than just the fame of a great explorer. His journey down the Congo River had alerted him to the fact that here lay a region ripe for commercial exploitation. The Congo River, for all its mythical isolation, was in fact easily navigable for most of its length, and it offered therefore the opportunity to any stout-hearted nation to exploit an almost unimaginable wealth of gold and ivory, the staples of African trade that had made so many fortunes already.

With a flair for self-aggrandizement, Stanley began immediately to lecture and publish, beginning in England but wending his way through all the great capitals of Europe. His mission was simply to urge any and all who would listen to seize the opportunity to claim the Congo and win for themselves not only the prodigious economic prize on offer, but also a great moral opportunity to stamp out the last embers of the East African Slave Trade, then flourishing in anonymity in the dark heart of Africa.

A picture of slaves captured from the Congo on an Arab slave trader

At that point in history, however, the general European mood was conservative, and in Britain in particular, under the leadership of Prime Minister Benjamin Disraeli, there was a notable disinterest in assuming any additional fiscal responsibility in Africa. And although there was only standing room at every lecture and his books flew off the shelves, there was a conspicuous coolness all over Europe over the question of annexation.

In one very minor European capital, however, Stanley's exhortations were being taken very seriously. King Leopold II, titular monarch of Belgium, was taking very careful note, and through emissaries and intermediaries, he was subtly pursuing Stanley.

King Leopold II of Belgium

Leopold emerges from the pages of history as a curious character. He was a member of a privileged clique of European monarchs, bereft of power but rich, indulgent, and indolent. Leopold certainly availed himself of all the pleasures of court life, but he was also shrewd, astonishingly competent, and avaricious to an almost unimaginable degree. His initial interest in foreign real estate was imperial, insofar as he desired on behalf of Belgium the main accoutrements of a first-rate power, which were, of course, foreign estates and colonies. He was, however, unable to move the Belgian parliament to act in accordance, the conservative belief perhaps being that Belgium could not afford to compete on that level. Belgium was a small

European nation, existing between major and, at times, belligerent powers, and as such, it quietly went about its business with a determination not to rock the European boat.

Despairing of that avenue, Leopold next began to try and acquire a foreign colony on his own account. He sought at various times to buy a province of Argentina, to lease the Philippines from Spain, and to acquire from the French a quarter of Indo-China. None of these schemes amounted to much, but then, abruptly, in 1877, an upstart explorer by the name of Henry Morton Stanley emerged from the mouth of the Congo River, proclaiming to the world that here lay the next great El Dorado. This, Leopold realized, was his opportunity. He held his breath as Stanley toured the capitals of Europe, and as one by one they politely declined his importuning, he allowed his own interest to be known.

Once the fanfare of Stanley's celebrity had died down somewhat and realizing that he was unlikely to succeed where he most hoped, he settled for the second-class option and accepted an invitation to visit Leopold at the Royal Palace Laeken. Here he was lavishly feted and entertained, until, in due course, Leopold made him an offer. If Stanley would return to the Congo and begin establishing on Leopold's behalf the necessary infrastructure to conduct trade — those being a railway line around the first rapids and thereafter river stations and— this would establish Leopold's *prima petition* over the Congo, and for his efforts, Stanley would be amply rewarded.

To this, Stanley agreed, and in due course he set off back to the Congo. This left Leopold with the ticklish diplomatic conundrum of securing international recognition. Certain features of Stanley's account had caught his attention, and one was the rampant proliferation of slavery on the upper reaches of the Congo, originating from the slave markets of Zanzibar and supplying a thriving black market in slaves across the Arab world.[1] This, he decided, would be his *cause célèbre*. His opening move was simply to announce to the world his intention of forming an international organization to combat slavery in the Congo, which, in an age of abolition, was an extremely potent and shrewd maneuver. To satisfy the more mercantile interests of the ruling classes of Europe, he offered up the Congo River as an international free trade zone, and to capture the interests of the United States, he suggested the Congo as a destination to repatriate free-born blacks and freed slaves.

In combination, all of this represented an unstoppable momentum, and displaying enormous ability and a masterful grasp of diplomatic maneuver, Leopold was able to secure primary rights over the territory of the Congo River catchment, a portion of the globe more than three times the size of France. By any standards, this was a monumental coup, and by the time the other European powers woke up to precisely what was underway, it was too late the arrest the momentum.

---

[1] The East African Slave Trade had by then been outlawed, but it continued on the back of the ivory trade. Slaves were captured in the first instance by Swahili traders to portage ivory to the coast, and were sold thereafter as a secondary commodity.

Of all the issues on the agenda as delegates gathered in Berlin in 1884, foremost was the Congo question. The matter was debated, and although deeply troubled by the potential consequences, recognition was eventually afforded to Leopold's claim to the Congo. And so, the Congo Free State came into being, a private fiefdom of Leopold II of Belgium and arguably one of the most cynical and exploitative colonial regimes across the European spectrum. The truth of this would not immediately come to light, and the high-minded proclamations that accompanied the formation of Leopold's colony were taken at face value. However, it was of profound importance was to ensure that nothing like it could happen again, and central to the agenda of the conference, which lasted almost a year, was to establish certain ground rules governing the future European partition of Africa.

Of these, three are most noteworthy. The first was that the annexation of any territory in Africa by any European power would not be formally recognized without a clear display of effective occupation and administration. Second, no such annexation could proceed without a formal request for protection on the part of an indigenous leader or monarch responsible for that territory. Such a plea for protection would be required to be submitted to treaty and be ascribed with the seal, mark, or signature of that king. The third rule, which could perhaps be better described as a convention, required that in the event of a European war, the territories, protectorates, and colonies acquired under the terms of the conference's General Act would remain neutral.

The Start of the War

By the 20th century, warfare was nothing new to the European powers, especially when it came to fighting each other. Conflicts had been a mainstay on the European continent for over two millennia. Even after the Napoleonic wars had enveloped Europe in large scale war for nearly 20 years in the 19th century, the Europeans' imperialism continued unabated. It would take the devastation of World War I to shock Europe and jolt the world's superpowers out of their imperialistic tendencies.

After Napoleon and the French were was finally defeated in 1815 by a coalition of European nations, Europe went about their most serious attempt to create peace on the continent. Even before the fighting had ended, most major European powers had been meeting in Vienna and established a congress in 1814. A series of agreements were reached between the coalition and the defeated French to end the fighting.

However, the Europeans continued to conduct business as usual, spending much of the 19th century engaged in imperialism across the world. The natural response of the European nations was to establish alliances that would maintain at least a balance of power. In 1873, German chancellor Otto van Bismarck reached an alliance with Austria-Hungary's despot and the Russian czar. The French signed alliances with Britain and Russia, who had left its previous alliance over tension brought about by Austria-Hungary's intervention in the Balkans. By then,

Italy had joined the German alliance.

Although a couple of wars were fought on the European continent during the 19th century, an uneasy peace was mostly maintained across the continent for most of the 19th century after Napoleon. Despite this ostensible peace, the Europeans were steadily conducting arms races against each other, particularly Germany and Britain. Britain had been the world's foremost naval power for centuries, but Germany hoped to build its way to naval supremacy. The rest of Europe joined in on the arms race in the decade before the war started.

With Europe anticipating a potential war, all that was missing was a conflagration. That would start in 1908, when Austria-Hungary annexed Bosnia-Herzegovina in the Balkan Peninsula, drawing it into dispute with Russia. Moreover, this upset neighboring Serbia, which was an independent nation. From 1912-1913, a conflict was fought in the Balkans between the Balkan League and the Ottoman Empire, resulting in the weakening of the Ottoman Turks. After the First Balkan War, a second was fought months later between members of the Balkan League itself.

The final straw came June 28, 1914, when a Serbian assassinated Archduke Franz Ferdinand, the heir to the throne of Austria-Hungary, in Sarajevo, Bosnia. Although there had been explicit displays of commiseration and sympathy for Austria and widespread condemnation of Serbia's actions in the immediate aftermath of Franz Ferdinand's assassination, the attitude of the great powers towards Austria as the notional aggrieved party became substantially chillier as Austria insisted on virtually bullying Serbia over the whole affair. The British Prime Minister, Asquith, complained in an official letter that Serbia had no hope of appeasing Austria diplomatically, and that the terms of the July Ultimatum would've been impossible to meet even if Serbia was willing to do so. Indeed, it appears as though such an exacting document had been drafted precisely because Serbia didn't have a hope of complying, even if they had so wished, and thus Austria-Hungary would be able to go to war and punish them properly for the outrage perpetrated against their royal family.

The Archduke and his family in 1910

Contemporary media illustration depicting the assassination

A propaganda cartoon after the assassination that asserted "Serbia must die!"

100 years removed from the assassination, it might be unfair to say that it caused World War I, but it certainly started it. Historians still debate whether the Great War would have occurred even if Franz Ferdinand and Sophie lived out their lives in peace and comfort, but many believe that while it might've come months or years down the road, it was inevitable. The tangled web of alliances at cross-purposes, the growing diplomatic tensions, the arms race, the belligerence of newly powerful states such as Germany, the interference in other sovereign countries' affairs, and the relentless politicking all pointed towards one tragic outcome.

As for the parties themselves, it's apparent that much of the blame can be shouldered by the Serbian government. To this day, it's still unclear how much the King and Prime Minister knew about the plots and actions carried out, but they were obviously privy to the official communications that involved the conspirators, which included the head of Serbian Military Intelligence. Furthermore, it was the Serbian government, not the Black Hand (which at that point was virtually synonymous with Dimitrijević and Military Intelligence in any case) that provided Princip, Grabež, Cubrilovic, and the other conspirators with their firearms, explosives, training, and the means to cross the border into Bosnia. The People's Defence, the clandestine group within Bosnia, had been almost completely taken over by Serbian Military Intelligence and was effectively acting as a shell organization. Government officials from several different agencies had colluded with the conspirators on many occasions, with the end result that on the day of the assassination, the assassins were in place, suitably organized, well-armed for their purpose, and ready for action. At the same time, there are strong indications that several officials within the Serbian government (with or without sanction from on high) attempted to warn their

Austro-Hungarian counterparts of what was to come.

Another country that must bear a share of the blame is Russia. According to the confession given by Dimitrijević at the end of his 1917 trial in Salonika, Russia was fully aware of his activities, and he had no reason to lie at that point. Indeed, according to Dimitrijević, the Russian Military Attachè in Belgrade had guaranteed that Russia would stand with Serbia against Austria-Hungary in the event that the operation was compromised, and that he had received funds from Russia to carry out the assassination. An investigative journalist attempting to uncover the truth received a fairly unconvincing testimony from the Russian Military Attachè, who denied any involvement. The Russian Military Attachè claimed that his Assistant had been in charge during the period leading up to the assassination, and that Dimitrijević never apprised him of his plans or intentions. It has also been suggested that the Tsar, or at the very least the Prime Minister, were aware of a forthcoming attempt against Franz Ferdinand's life and were not opposed to it happening. Russia had a vested interest both in weakening the Austro-Hungarian Empire and in destabilizing its hold on the Balkans as this might well potentially give it access to the strategically invaluable Mediterranean ports without having to pass through the Turkish-controlled Bosphorus and Dardanelles straits, which hampered its attempts to increase its naval power outside of the Black Sea.

Even Austria-Hungary, despite being the aggrieved party, had a hand in what followed the assassination. The Austro-Hungarian military had resisted many attempts at pacification with Serbia, including policies advocated by Franz Ferdinand himself, and it continued to pursue a policy of aggressive saber-rattling. Furthermore, the Governor of Bosnia, Oskar Potiorek, was a rigid and stubborn individual who viewed Slavic patriots as a national security threat and ruthlessly punished them accordingly, further inflaming anti-Austrian sentiment in a newly created province that required the most delicate of management rather than hamfisted pacification attempts. His refusal to countenance the use of improperly dressed troops to shield Franz Ferdinand and his halting of the motorcade in a vulnerable position near the bank of the river were symptomatic of his stubbornness, and his decision to remain idle while Sarajevo tore apart the homes of hundreds of innocent Serbs is evidence of his poor character.

Ironically, one of the few people who had no blame in what was to come was Franz Ferdinand himself. A choleric individual with the typical Austrian aristocrat's condescending attitude towards the subordinate Hungarian population, he was nonetheless no more prejudiced than many during his time and a great deal less than most; after all, he married a woman from the Czech aristocracy who was beneath his station. On top of that, his attitude towards Serbia and the Slavic issue was remarkably conciliatory for someone in his position. He went to his death unwittingly even after bravely continuing his public appearance despite having a hand grenade hurled at him. It is unfortunate for Franz Ferdinand that his birth and position made him an ideal target, but as history and fate would have it, he was simply the right man in the wrong place at the wrong time.

Though nobody can know for sure, it's altogether possible that World War I would have still broken out even if Franz Ferdinand had not been murdered. Regardless of events in the Balkans, Germany was already bellicose, France and Austria were concerned and involved, Russia was outwardly aggressive but also dealing with internal dissatisfaction, Italy was poised on the brink, and Britain was desperate to remain aloof but committed to its continental allies and a host of smaller countries clamoring for independence. Europe was too explosive to be rescued by any but the best of diplomats, if at all.

A Bold Scheme

On April 21, 1915, Admiral Sir Henry Jackson, in charge of the Royal Navy's operations, prepared himself in his spacious admiralty office for a brief appointment with a man named John R. Lee. His notes indicated that Lee was a retired military officer and African hunter who wished to present a proposal to unlock the balance of naval power in Africa. Admiral Jackson had, in truth, given very little thought to the African theater. Various little operations were underway here and there on the continent, but on the whole, he had bigger fish to fry, and he had only agreed to meet John Lee because the latter would simply not take no for answer.

Admiral Jackson

The African theater of World War I was, in fact, surprisingly volatile. A major campaign in German South West Africa was lumbering to a conclusion - the Allies had taken German Kamerun, and Allied forces were now preparing to take to the field against the Germans in East Africa. The Germans, on the whole, were working out a successful strategy of keeping the theater active to divert Allied manpower and resources away from Europe, believing that victory would be won on the Western Front, and that upon that victory, the contested African territories would be German regardless of who held them at the end of the war.

When the door of his office was presently opened and John Lee ushered in, Admiral Jackson was introduced to a sinuous man in his 50s, tall, sunburned, and fit. With the pleasantries disposed of, the two men sat, and Admiral Jackson glanced sharply at his pocket watch before he looked up and smiled. Lee understood, and he got straight to the point. On the burgundy leather desk between them, he spread out a map of Africa and pointed to a spot in the south and center of the continent. This, he explained, was Lake Tanganyika, a vast inland waterway some 450 miles long and 45 miles wide. It was bordered on the east by German East Africa and on the west by the Belgian Congo, and at the southern tip, the British held a tiny enclave. One need only look at a map, he went on, to appreciate the strategic advantage of the lake in such a sprawling and difficult theater. From the point of view of transport and as a defensive buffer, it was incomparable. The key to the entire East African Campaign, he insisted, was control of this lake.

Lee sat back, allowing Admiral Jackson a moment or two to digest these details before he went on. The German Imperial Navy currently operated two warships on the lake: the SMS *Hedwig von Wissmann*, a 60-ton steam launch, somewhat top-heavy, and relatively lightly armed, and the SMS *Kingani*, configured similarly, but weighing in at 40 tons. Moreover, his information was that the Germans were putting the finishing touches on the assembly of a much larger ship, the SMS *Graf von Götzen*, 1,500 tons displacement and 240 feet bow to stern. She was well-armed and fast, and once on the water, German command of the lake would be absolute.

The SMS *Hedwig von Wissmann*

With that in mind, Lee noted that Allied forces were building to the north and south of German East Africa, preparing a major offensive for the spring of 1916, and that a Royal Naval blockade had effectively sealed access to the colony. Thus, British naval dominance of Lake Tanganyika would complete the encirclement, and German defeat would simply be a matter of time. If the

Royal Navy moved quickly, there was still time to catch the Germans napping and seize strategic control of the lake, but time was of the essence.

Admiral Jackson sat back in his chair. He was a man indisposed to superficial conversation. The point was taken, he said, and so what did Lee propose? The difficulty, of course, lay in how to get British ships to a lake in the middle of Africa during a war in which the enemy controlled the only railway. Ships built *in situ* on the lake shore would be destroyed as fast as they were assembled. The trick would be to transport light and effective gunboats overland from the Cape, through Belgian territory, and then launch them on the western shore, fully assembled, fully armed, and ready to go into action.

Why not simply launch them in British territory, at the southern tip of the lake? That would place them out of range of German port facilities, and besides that, no completed railway was available to transport the gunboats within reasonable overland haulage distance of the lake. Any battles would need to take place in the center of the lake. A far better option would be to utilize the great north railway and to launch the boats in Belgian territory mid-way up the lake.

Lee had traveled and hunted through that region since his commando riding days in the Anglo/Boer War. He knew the country well, he assured Admiral Jackson, and he knew the people. It was his opinion that such boats could feasibly be transported by rail, river, and haulage to Lake Tanganyika. It would be the last thing that the Germans would expect, and with the element of surprise, the battle was as good as won.

Admiral Jackson listened closely to all of this, glancing not once at the clock on the mantle, and by the end of the appointed hour, he was entirely convinced. A proposal was put to the Board of Admiralty, and under Admiral Jackson's personal piloting, it was granted early approval. It was further submitted to the Colonial Office and the Army Council, both of which granted their provisional approvals. Lee was informed, and the bureaucratic arm of the Royal Navy applied itself to attending to the details.

Lee was given the task of identifying appropriate boats for the operation, and he was granted a certain amount of leeway in selecting his own senior staff, all of whom, including himself, would be commissioned at various ranks into the Royal Naval Volunteer Reserve. The operation was only superficially a naval operation, insofar as its major element comprised a land expedition that favored men of Lee's cut, and so the anomaly of landsmen leading a Royal Naval expedition would simply have to be tolerated. Lee, however, could not command the expedition, nor a Royal Navy fleet for that matter, once it was on the water, so while it might simply have been an honorary position during the early stages of the expedition, it was essential that a Royal Navy man be in ostensible command. A search then began of available Royal Navy personnel to take formal command of the operation.

This was no easy task, because every good man was engaged in some capacity. The general organization of the operation was placed under the overall command of Admiral Sir David Gamble—well named, some were apt to remark—and it was he who was charged with locating and appointing a commander to what was now formally known as the Naval Africa Expedition.

Lee, in the meantime, set off in search of the boats for the expedition, and he found precisely what he was looking for in the yards of John Thornycroft & Company Limited, located on the Thames River in lower Twickenham. A single, mahogany-built, 40 foot motor launch was currently under construction on behalf of the Greek Air Force. Eight boats of a similar model had been built, all serving as tenders in various locations, and this was the last. Lee immediately commandeered it on Royal Navy authority, and after some research, he located its sister ship, identical in almost every way, operating as a tender in Dundee. This too he promptly commandeered and had transported to London. Both boats were powered by identical 100-horsepower gasoline engines, each driving twin screws, rendering the boats capable of a highly respectable top speed of 19 knots.

Sir David Gamble, meanwhile, in his search for a commander, toured the various branches of the Royal Navy, eventually identifying a furloughed Royal Marine Corps Major currently attached to the Royal Navy Intelligence division. Gamble visited the offices of the Intelligence branch and there plotted out the essentials of the operation, vaguely stabbing a map of Africa with his finger and scratching his chin as he sought to identify which of the great lakes was Lake Tanganyika. The Royal Marine Major picked up the map and perused it thoughtfully for fully five minutes before handing it back to Gamble with the judgment that the mission was impossible.

The two shook hands, and the RMC Major left the room. Gamble remained, however, still scratching his chin, when suddenly, from the corner of the room, there came a light cough. Gamble had hardly noticed a second man seated at one of a handful desks in the room. The man introduced himself as Lieutenant Commander Geoffrey Spicer-Simson, currently attached to the Intelligence division in a clerical capacity, and that if such a vacancy existed, he would be more than willing to consider it. For a moment, Gamble did not know what to make of it. What he knew for certain was that only gross incompetence could explain why a Royal Naval Commander would be seated behind a desk in London in the middle of a war. Since no one else would take the job, however, the matter was put before the expedition planning committee for approval. Jackson applied the logic that the position was titular anyway since Lee would lead the expedition, so there was no reason why Commander Spicer-Simson should not be given the command, and his approval was granted.

Spicer-Simson had a poor reputation in the Royal Navy, but as interesting as the expedition might have been, there can be no doubt, bearing mind the sheer weight of naval iron afloat on the oceans at that time, that it was a sideshow. Thus, if Commander Spicer-Simson was in the habit of losing ships, then the further that he could be kept out of the way of commanding them would obviously be money well spent.

Spicer-Simson

If, on the other hand, an unconventional operation required an unconventional commander, then Gamble succeeded spectacularly. History tends to paint Commander Spicer-Simson as a blunt, abrasive, unintelligent, and braggartly character, with such a host of disagreeable attributes that his incompetence could quite easily be nothing more than an invention of his enemies. The facts, however, tend to disagree, but sometimes the right man is in the right place at the right time.

What is certain is that Commander Spicer-Simson was a bold, well-built, strong, and aggressive man. He was antagonistic and condescending towards his juniors, to women in general, and service staff in particular. He was also guilty of perhaps the most unpardonable of all sins in an institutionalized hierarchy: he gave an impression of over-familiarity with his seniors. His career, however, had he confined himself only to social failures such as these, might well have survived, but no Royal Naval career has long survived a charge of incompetence and certainly not if that charge is accompanied by conspicuous damage to His Majesty's property. In the case of Commander Spicer-Simson, not one, but two such charges were on the record, and after that, a man might consider himself lucky to be allowed to push papers around at a general use desk in the Admiralty offices.

Born in Hobart, Tasmania in January 1876, Spicer-Simson was one of five children of a British gold-sovereign dealer and the daughter of an English country clergyman. At the age of 14, he enlisted in the Royal Navy and showed considerable early promise. Rising rapidly through the ranks, he gained a promotion to acting sub-lieutenant in February 1896, moving then into surveying as a specialization and serving for a time on the Royal North Borneo Boundary Commission of 1901.

Promotion to a command position, however, was slow in coming. This was probably, notwithstanding tremendous ambition, simply because he was so consistently disagreeable. When at last he was granted the coveted appointment of captain of a destroyer, he ran his first ship into the side of an American liberty ship, sinking it and killing one crew member. A board of inquiry sat, Spicer-Simson was court-martialed, and for several years thereafter he languished dockside on watch-keeping duties. Then, between 1905 and 1908, the monotony of this was relieved by a brief posting to China, where he made the first triangulated survey of the Yangtze River, and from there he headed to West Africa, where he commanded a Royal Navy survey ship.

At the outbreak of World War I, with naval officers in short supply, he served a brief tour on board a contraband control vessel before he was favored once again with a promotion to Senior Naval Officer of the Downs Boarding Flotilla. This placed him in command of two Royal Navy gunboats and six boarding tugs operating out of the small, east English port of Ramsgate. The story of how and why has never been entirely articulated, but somehow the young commander was able to lose one of his gunboats in harbor when it was torpedoed in broad daylight by a German U-boat. He was removed once again from his command, and hence, as Sir David Gamble was imploring someone—anyone—to take command of an expedition to Africa, Geoffrey Spicer Simson happened to be sitting at a desk within earshot.

Mimi and *Toutou*

"Never trust a bullying braggart in a skirt." – Giles Foden

The essence of Lee's plan was that the two boats would be transported by ship from Tilbury in London to Cape Town, and from there, they would be rail freighted the 2,700 miles to the rail depot of Fungurume in the Katanga region of what was then the Belgian Congo. Fungurume lies some 120 miles to the northwest of present-day Lubumbashi, which was in 1915 known as Elizabethville, the regional capital of Katanga. The Katanga region was then the center of an emerging mining industry, already well established to the south of the international frontier in Northern Rhodesia, the future Zambia.[2] Fungurume was the site of numerous mines, and it was to there that the railway extended and no further. The Great North Railway line ran from Cape Town to Bulawayo in what was then Southern Rhodesia, but which is now Zimbabwe. From there, it plied northwards to Livingstone and Lusaka—then in Northern Rhodesia, or the modern

---

[2] The Zambian Copper Belt and the Katanga Copper mines are part of same broad mineral region.

state of Zambia—and from there, via the Copper Belt, to the southern Congolese province of Katanga. The terminus, of course, was Fungurume.

North of that, as is not entirely untrue today, there was very little civilization. Small pockets of the indigenous population were widely scattered, while isolated Belgian administrative settlements punctuated thousands of square miles of unmapped and barely explored territory. It was, as it remains, a wild and intensely beautiful region, home of some of the most remote wilderness areas left in Africa, and it is still largely trackless.

It was through this region that Lee proposed to haul the boats 120 miles, reaching a short, regional railhead that served a small mine at the settlement of Sunkisia. From there, it would make a brief 15-mile journey to the banks of the Lualaba River.

The Lualaba is an important regional waterway, the headwaters of the Congo River and a navigable regional transport route. Lee proposed that the two boats be floated downriver 200 miles to the town of Kabalo before another 200 miles of railway line would transport them to Albertville, today known as Kalemie, and then to a small Belgian port on the west shore of Lake Tanganyika. There they would be launched in readiness for the second phase of the expedition.

Lee submitted various recommendations for officers, four of whom were approved and commissioned at various ranks into the Royal Naval Volunteer Reserve. In addition, nine navy ratings were supplied by the Royal Navy, and Lee was authorized to hire no more than 300 natives for portage and the heavy work of cutting and shoring up the road to be built between Fungurume and Sunkisia.

Meanwhile, on April 26, 1915, Spicer-Simson was confirmed as Acting-Commander of the expedition, which entitled him after a long furlough to wear the coveted gilded oak leaves, although he was given to understand from the onset that this was Lee's expedition and that his appointment had been solely to satisfy Royal Naval protocol.

Lee then left in advance of the main party to begin the preliminary work of preparing a road between Fungurume and Sunkisia, leaving Commander Spicer-Simson to complete the refitting of the two boats and the final preparations before the main body of the expedition would follow a few months later. With him, he took an amiable journalist by the name of Frank Magee, a Fleet Street adventurer, as he was described by the expedition's physician, Doctor H. M. Hanschell, who was entered onto the expedition's register as "Petty Officer Writer".

The launches, in the meantime, were numbered "one" and "two", and it was left to Commander Spicer-Simson to name them. His initial suggestion was RMS *Cat* and RMS *Dog*, which Admiral Jackson refused to approve. Spicer-Simson then returned with RMS *Mimi* and RMS *Toutou*, explaining that these were the same names in Parisian slang. Admiral Jackson seemed more willing to accept these names, perhaps having more pressing matters to deal with than the eccentric musings of a man whose back he was already anxious to see. In fact, as Spicer-Simson would later explain, *Mimi* and *Toutou* meant *Miaow* and *Bow-wow* in the same Parisian idiom, and thus they entered the register of Royal Navy ships.

The two launches were armed, each with a 3-pound gun on the bow, a Maxim aft, and light armor placed over the fuel tanks. The weight of arms and armor dropped the draft of the boats down almost a foot and reduced the top speed of each to 15 knots. This was still sufficient to outpace the German gunboats, however, which Lee had confirmed had a top speed of only 9 knots. Thornycroft built custom cradles for each, adapted to be used on rail cars and independently with solid rubber wheels. The boats were tested, their armaments fine-tuned, and various additional officers commissioned. Most of the personnel were not navy men, but engineers, miners, and railway men, all with various degrees of African experience, with gunners and seamen listed in the ratings.

The HMS *Mimi*

All of this was taking place as Lee and Magee made their way by rail from Cape Town to Fungurume, and in August 1915, with a large complement of native labor, they plunged into the wilderness and began the slow task of building the road. Initially, the going was slow but relatively easy. The landscape was of rolling woodland savannah, simple to traverse with a minimum of survey and with usually just the removal of an occasional tree or inconvenient undergrowth. Farther north, however, lay the southern finger of the Mitumba Mountains. This is a 300-mile complex of broken highlands and mountains that form a feature of the western Rift Valley, rising to two significant peaks: Mount Kahuzi (10,800 feet), and Mount Biéga (9,100 feet). The expedition would bypass the main range to the southeast, via a long and narrow ridge that today is part of Kundelungu National Park. The region lies at an average height of 6,000 feet, forming a plateau on either side of a sharply sloping series of ridges and gullies, heavily wooded and with light soils underfoot that only sparsely cover deep beds of hard volcanic rock.

Beyond this, however, lay one of Africa's most impenetrable and difficult regions. Lee now had to contemplate navigation through a vast landscape of wetlands, home to several shallow but significant lakes, among them Lakes Kabwe, Kabele, Mulenda, and Upempa. Even today, this is a sublimely beautiful corner of Africa, preserved from human impact mainly because of the sheer difficulty of accessing it. Dr. Livingstone wrote in praise of the majesty of this landscape, but he also remarked that it was the most challenging he had ever encountered.

A journal of the day-to-day progress of the journey was kept by Magee, and although the original has long since been lost, Magee wrote a detailed article on the expedition for *National Geographic Magazine* that appeared in a 1922 edition. His general tone throughout this narrative tends to be understated, but reading between the lines, the two men experienced an adventure on an epic scale that would seem hardly possible in the modern age. At the head of an army of native porters and laborers and supported by a lavishly funded official expedition, they were traversing a corner of Africa that few feet, European or African, had ever crossed before. "[G]oing ahead of the main body to select a route across the African bush," wrote Magee. "From the point where the boats would be taken off the train, it was important that a route be as free as possible from hills, gorges etc, yet close to water, should be chosen, as our boats were to be taken over this trail intact, each drawn by a [steam] traction engine. Great difficulty was experienced in finding a suitable route over which to make our road, owing to the hilly nature of the country, as well as long stretches of marshland, and breeding ground of malaria-carrying mosquitoes. But at last a route was selected and thousands of natives were recruited from adjacent villages to set to work under white supervision literally to carve a passage through the bush."

While this great adventure was underway, back in London, the main body of the expedition was preparing itself for its own long journey south to the Cape. Every member of the expedition had been sworn to secrecy, because if the Germans got wind of what was afoot, they would be prepared. No member of the expedition was permitted to reveal to family and friends that they were en route to Africa, and under no circumstances were any details of the operation to be revealed.

When Doctor Hanschell returned home that night and broke the news to his wife that he was leaving, and when he apologized for being unable to tell her precisely where and for what reason, she laughed and replied, "Oh didn't he [Commander Spicer-Simson] tell you dear, you're going to Lake Tanganyika via Rhodesia and the Congo River. [Mrs.] Amy Spicer-Simson telephoned me this afternoon and we had a long talk about it."

The Naval Africa Expedition

"The only traditions of the Royal Navy are Rum, Sodomy and the Lash." – Winston Churchill

Aboard the *Llandstephen Castle*, sometime in June 1915, Commander Spicer-Simson overheard members of the expedition's crew discussing the prospects of the operation and referring to it, as they had all along, as "Lee's Expedition." He gathered together the expedition members and ordered that no further references of this nature would be tolerated. The expedition was entitled the Naval Africa Expedition, and Spicer-Simson asserted that he was its commander. Long before Lee had approached the Admiralty with this scheme, he added, he had himself been contemplating a similar proposition, and there was no reason to suppose that, had Lee never appeared at the offices of Admiralty, he would not himself have had his own version of the plan approved.

With that, Spicer-Simson began disparaging Lee at every opportunity. He was, he implied, a drunkard with a reputation for unreliability. News had already reached him, he went on, that Lee had grossly insulted the Belgians, whose cooperation was vital, and that Lee was touring the bars and bordellos of Elizabethville revealing every detail of the expedition.

On one particular evening, as the *Llandstephen Castle* crossed the equator, a small group of passengers gathered on the port side rail were discussing the star constellations above. Spicer-Simson and Dr. Hanschell happened to stroll past. The Commander paused, listened to the speaker for a while, and then, correcting him on certain details, assumed the floor himself. He was in turn corrected, at which point he sternly reminded his audience that he was a Royal Naval officer, and as such he might be expected to know something about stars. The man spun on his heels and walked away, and as the two continued their walk, Doctor Hanschell remarked, "That was the Astronomer Royal of Cape Town.." "Is that so?" Spicer-Simson replied scathingly. "He'd make a damned poor Navigating Officer!"

And such was the pattern of the journey. Commander Spicer-Simson made enemies of everyone, in particular the ship's captain and crew, who he was prone to remind that under wartime conditions, he, as a Royal Navy commander, held de facto command of the ship. No one was sorry to see the expedition disembark at Cape Town on July 2, and no official valediction was offered. According to numerous memoirs, no single member of the crew or passenger list even said goodbye.

The *Mimi* and *Toutou* were unloaded in the meantime and secured on railway wagons in preparation for the journey north. Spicer-Simson disposed of the necessary official liaison and social communication about town, likely leaving in his wake as many shaking heads and ominous prognostications as he had aboard the *Llandstephen Castle*. Soon afterwards, the expedition boarded a special train and set off towards Bulawayo, where the Commander was scheduled to meet Colonel A.H.M. Edwards, Commandant-General of Allied forces in both Southern and Northern Rhodesia.

Here the expedition was temporarily halted. The Admiralty had received an unsolicited report from Belgian officials in the Congo that doubted the practicality of Lee's proposal to haul the boats across almost 200 miles of unmapped territory in the wilds of central Africa. Spicer-Simson was instructed to proceed no further until Lee had returned from his initial survey and could confirm that a practical route had been identified.

Spicer-Simson was billeted in the home of Colonel Edwards, and there he entertained the service elite of the colony with tales of his own achievements and a litany of scurrilous and wholly unsupported accusations against John Lee. Lee, at that moment, was nearing the end of his assignment, and although significant challenges would need to be overcome, he was confident that the project was viable. Spicer-Simson, meanwhile, sent ahead to Elizabethville Sub-Lieutenant Douglas Edward Hope, ostensibly to establish the status of Lee's mission, but unofficially to assassinate his character.

It was Hope who returned with reports of fictitious complaints leveled against Lee by the Belgian authorities and news of his drunkenness and unreliability. Hope traveled no farther inland than Elizabethville, and he certainly did not trace the route blazed by Lee and Magee, now almost complete, but simply dispatched a telegram directly to Colonel Edwards detailing all of these accusations. Others were sent to various local British officials, who compared notes and borrowed embellishments, adding for effect Spicer-Simson's lavish enlargements, all of which found their way in one form or another to the Admiralty.

The British High Commissioner at the Cape, receiving all of this disquieting news, ordered Spicer-Simson to proceed to Elizabethville in order to establish the facts for himself. This order was repeated by the Admiralty, with the additional instruction to the effect that if there was any truth in the allegations, Lee was to be dismissed immediately. Wasting no time, Commander Spicer-Simson set off. As he was en route, a telegram from Lee was received in Cape Town and copied to Salisbury and London. It originated from Elizabethville and indicated that Lee and Magee had returned from the interior and that Lee was happy to report the route that he had surveyed was practical. He lingered in Elizabethville, notified by cable from Cape Town that Spicer-Simson was on his way and that no further action was to be taken until the Commander had met and debriefed his subordinate.

Lee was rather surprised at the tone of the cable and his description as subordinate, but he was also entirely unaware of what had been taking place, so he did as he was instructed. As he waited, not a word was spoken about what he and Magee had achieved in just a few short months of labor. In future years, of course, Spicer-Simson would have much to say about his role in it, but it was Magee's later *National Geographic* piece that would offer the first and only reliable account of what must surely have been the adventure of a lifetime. In total, some 146 miles of road had been pushed forward through the wilderness, more-or-less by hand. According to Magee's own pen, "[The road] making, as it progressed, an unavoidable climb over a plateau 6,000 feet above sea level…where slopes were too steep they were [leveled] down. Bridges, constructed from timber growing on the spot, were thrown across river beds. Giant trees, when blocking our path, were uprooted with dynamite. Rocks and boulders were treated in a similar manner. Our single biggest problem was a dried up gorge, 40-yards wide and about 20-yards deep. This we completely filled with tree trunks. Thousands of trees were cleared out of the way."

Magee described an undertaking of such enormous proportions that it is hard to imagine the objective was simply the portage of two modest gunboats to the shores of a lake. It was entirely reasonable that Lee and Magee would have anticipated the gratitude of the Admiralty, the War Office, and the Empire as a whole for such selfless and self-sacrificing service. No doubt, as they cooled their heels in a hotel in Elizabethville, eagerly anticipating Spicer-Simson's arrival, that is what they expected.

A few days later, Commander Spicer-Simson arrived at the gabled railway station in Elizabethville, where he was met by Lee and escorted across the road to the hotel. There he settled in, and a few hours later, a meeting was held between him, Magee, and Lee in the bar of the hotel. The Commander sat patiently through the detailed description Lee delivered of all that had taken place in the months since the two had last met, including maps and comprehensive drawings and directions. It was not until all the survey maps and labor contracts had been handed over that he calmly announced to Lee that he had been accused of insulting the Belgians while drunk and generally revealing details of the expedition to all and sundry, and he was therefore ordered to return to Cape Town to await disciplinary action. One can easily imagine that Lee would have stared at his ostensible superior, wondering if it was a joke. When it became clear, however, that it was no joke, Lee realized immediately what was behind it all. He made no protest, but simply collected himself, stood up, and left the room.

Magee, however, who had in the months of shared experience grown very close to Lee, protested vehemently on his behalf. If information had reached the Germans, which was not actually true despite Spicer-Simson's accusations, the Germans would not know for sure what was taking place until the first shots were fired at them across the lake. What other conclusion would they reach when intelligence was confirmed that a road was under construction from Fungurume to Lake Tanganyika?

As other members of the expedition arrived with the two launches, a majority tended to agree. There was absolutely no evidence of any impropriety on Lee's behalf, and certainly no Belgian official could be found to confirm that Lee had insulted the Belgian flag. Moreover, if the Germans knew that an expedition was en route to the lake, then so did half of Cape Town. John Lee was obviously highly regarded in this region, and there quite clearly was no basis upon which to engineer his disgrace and dismissal. The Commander, however, was unmoved, and his motivations were entirely transparent. With few exceptions, he had not been particularly popular among the crew, but now he was in command of an expedition that despised him almost to a man. Lee was commiserated with, and a great deal of morbid drinking took place until, in the end, Lee collected his wages from the expedition's Paymaster and left town. He made his way from Elizabethville to Cape Town and there faced a brief inquiry. No record of any action against him exists, however, and thereafter he simply faded away into history, never to reappear.

A Magnificent Journey

"No one will pay you for planning an expedition." – Sir Ranulph Fiennes

Under a dark cloud, the Naval Africa Expedition set off towards Fungurume, the terminus of the Great North Railway. Here the two launches were de-trained, prepared in cradles, and secured to their custom-made carriages for the start of the overland phase. With Lee gone, it now fell to Frank Magee to guide the expedition along the recently constructed route. Labor was assembled, the oxen were marshaled, and the two steam tractors checked over and repaired. In the distance, brooding and silent in the fresh and dry atmosphere of winter, the Mitumba Mountains marked a barrier between the open country of the south and the marshes, wetlands, and rivers of the north. The Naval Africa Expedition truly had begun, and each man must have felt the keen sense that he was stepping forward into something unique.

The events that followed were first written about and published in the official report of the expedition, which is neutral and reveals only the sequential facts of what took place. Later, Spicer-Simson himself wrote the occasional essay and lectured from time to time, but those were taken with a pinch of salt. The most colorful and accessible account remains Frank Magee's 1922 *National Geographic* piece. This, again, is quite sterile, and although it side steps the human drama as much as possible, it seems constantly to marvel at the consistent triumph of the absurd over geography and nature.

There is, however, no derogatory mention at all of Commander Spicer-Simson. Through his own and other accounts, Frank Magee seems to have been a very even-tempered, pleasant, and amusing companion, and if there was one member of the crew least likely to be offended by the Commander, it would have been Magee. There were one or two sycophants who clung to him, but for the remainder, Spicer-Simson established a patronizing and antagonistic attitude towards his subordinates. Needless to say, with Lee out of the way and now far beyond recall, his multiple personality defects were unrestrained. He was universally despised, and he succeeded in his leadership of the expedition for no other reason than that Lee had prepared the way ahead of him so expertly.

It is also true that everyone was invested in the scheme with or without Spicer-Simson. This was one of the great epic adventures of the war, it was well-resourced, and they were part of it. Behind them, in the bars of Elizabethville, every townsman had been intimately appraised of the objectives of the expedition by its own commander, and the odds were running to 100:1 that the whole thing would travel no more than 50 miles.

With a flash of accidental genius, Spicer-Simson had created a smokescreen. Intelligence was by then streaming back to German East African headquarters from everywhere that the expedition had so far landed, but it was so outrageous that the Germans did not believe a word of it and kept trying to unearth what the real objective of the road was.

The expedition, meanwhile, proceeded entirely as planned for the first phase. It comprised a rotating compliment of about 300 native porters, stockmen, herdsmen, and woodcutters. The two steam tractors were standard models built by the thousand by Burrell's of Thetford, restored examples of which can still be seen in museums, archives, and scrap-yards all across the old British Empire. They were coal fired, but there was no coal, so they consumed enormous amounts of firewood. Equipment and supplies were all carried by porter or ox wagon, and of course, other oddments of livestock followed the local members, who were usually also followed by their wives and children. Ultimately, the expedition became a moving village.

Here, in an unexpected way, Commander Spicer-Simson found affection and kinship. He was as high-handed and patronizing towards the indigenous members and followers as he was to the British crew, and yet he was highly regarded among them. He was fond of native children, and he always had one or two close alongside him. He was also generous with gifts and treats, constantly giving them to kids and their mothers. People came from miles around to visit and watch the spectacle of two steam tractors hissing and shrieking, with the ever-present thud of axes on wood and the rumble of wheels and hooves. No one was ever prepared to swear that the steam tractors helped in any way, but they gave the expedition its circus atmosphere and embellished the prestige of its leader, whose outbursts and eccentricities simply added to the sense of theater.

Magee recorded the arrival on the scene of a local chief, dressed in an old British military tunic, a pair of white spats worn over bare feet, an opera hat, and a pink sunshade. The Commander greeted him with appropriate ceremony, and an audience was held, all of which tickled Magee's humor and his sense of the absurd. Author Giles Foden, whose book *Mimi and Toutou's Big Adventure* dwells in some detail on Spicer-Simson's peculiarities, observed of how this was viewed by the natives: "The story of Spicer's mission went through ever more fantastic permutations, mile after mile, beat after beat, until, by the time it reached the Holo-holo living on the lakeshore, Spicer had been elevated to something like a god."

In Magee's eyes at least, Spicer-Simson was entirely rehabilitated. John Lee is recorded by his pen as having retired from the expedition because of "sunstroke and fever." He describes the Commander, during the more rough phases of the expedition, as "setting a fine example" and "encouraging his officers and men with a kindly word" It's likely his words were less than encouraging, but there is no doubt he set a fine example. His energy was demonic, and no obstacle was too large to tackle. In the blue distance loomed the escarpment that the expedition would soon have to cross, but for the moment, on a dry expanse of savannah, his difficulty was in finding enough water to keep the steam engines turning. On several occasions, men and animals were denied their rations to keep the iron beasts watered.

Lieutenant Alfred Edward Wainwright, a Rhodesian colonist recruited en route, was given authority to search for water, and he returned a few hours later with a small army of women, each with a pot of water on their heads. Several journeys were made, and as the job was done, the great machines hissed back to life, cheered on their slow ambulation north by the population of several surrounding villages.

The real business, however, began as the expedition entered the foothills of the Mitumba Mountains. The flank of the escarpment was clad in forest, and heavy clouds gathered every afternoon, presaging rain. These were critical moments, as a single rainstorm would have stopped the expedition in its tracks. It was laborious enough dragging the two gunboats on their trolleys and cradles up the steep ravines and around deep gullies without the addition of mud and rain, which would have made it impossible.

Under these conditions, the expedition achieved just a few miles a day, using one and sometimes both tractors to haul the boats up in turns. Animal power was added, and winches, cross-winches, and windlasses were used to keep the cradles steady as they were edged around tight corners and over stream beds and rivers. Soon the point was reached when the tractors could no longer move forward. The labor of providing wood and the increasingly steep terrain simply made them impractical. Animal power was now required, and within a few days, a train of draft oxen arrived, driven by a tall and taciturn Dutchman wearing a British Army slouch hat. Lee, predicting that this would happen, had requisitioned several draft teams in South Africa and arranged for their transport north.

The engines were winched back down the side of the hill, after which they set off back to the mine or farm from which they had been requisitioned. Teams of oxen were then harnessed up to the cradles, and with cracking whips and a great deal of bellowing and hue and cry, the slow journey resumed. The caravan groaned up the side of the escarpment, arriving eventually on level ground on September 8, 1915.

For a few miles, over an undulating landscape of grassland and high plains, the caravan moved easily, but soon enough, the lead animals came to an abrupt halt, and there ahead was the trailing edge of the escarpment and the vast Lualaba River valley, flat and forbidding below. The descent was cautious and slow, but again Lee had left an expertly constructed track for the expedition to follow. When level ground was reached, there remained just a short isthmus to be crossed by rail before reaching the shallow banks of the Lualaba River. There, the *Mimi* and *Toutou* were unloaded, their cradles stowed on board, and they, at last, took to the water. Magee recalled, "I will not go into any more details of that memorable bush trek. After long days of toil and many qualms as to whether our destination would ever be attained, we eventually reached Sankisia, a railway depot about 18 miles from the River Lualaba."

The Lualaba is the headwater of the Congo River, one of the greatest inland waterways in Africa, and as the two launches were unleashed from their cradles and set on its placid surface, the expedition found itself in new and entirely different terrain. The Lualaba flows north through 70 miles of malarial wetlands, the low horizon unbroken, merging with one or more of the lakes, until it narrows once again and commences its long journey north to merge with the Congo.

The tiny port of Bukama was a river depot serving the railhead for a short line running inland to a mine. Shallow drafted steamers moved periodically up and down downriver, pausing here and there at scattered villages to collect people and produce. The *Mimi* and *Toutou* joined this intermittent traffic, although both were pulling drafts too deep to avoid running aground often in the shallow channels that laced through the marshlands. On the open water, it was easier, and for a while, the two boats were taken on board a steamboat, captained by a Belgian skipper who the doctor described as drunken and emotionally tortured. They passed a rusting barge aground in the middle of a shallow lake, where lived the lake pilot in a home surrounded by water. His blond wife, serene in her isolation, played piano at sunset, captivating the imagination of Magee, who wrote wistfully in later years of that enigmatic memory.

The river journey was some 350 miles down the Lualaba River to meet with the last stretch of rail. Once through the wetlands, the river narrowed and deepened, and a steady progress was made as the languid hours and days passed. Magee described an average day during this part of the journey: "This 'pleasant voyage' was a grueling business. We were baked alive during the day, and tormented at night by all the flying pests of the Congo…we camped ashore every night and always made an effort to get our evening meal over before darkness set in… [otherwise] a plate of soup, a few minutes after being placed on the table, became a seething mass of floundering insect life."

The 17-day river journey ended at the settlement of Kabalo, a river port on the Lualaba that was linked by rail to the lake *entrepôt* of Albertville, nowadays known as Kalemie. All that remained was a final, 200-mile railway journey that was completed without mishap, and as luck would have it, the two gunboats arrived at their destination just as the first rains of the season began to fall.

Thus ended one of the most daring and unusual expeditions at the twilight of the age of discovery. Whatever might have been his defects—and they certainly were many, and more would yet be revealed—Commander George Spicer-Simson had successfully completed the most difficult part of his commission.

What remained now was to establish naval dominance on the lake, but much had happened in the theater of war in the months since the expedition had left London. By then, the Germans were significantly more battle ready on the lake than had been previously thought, and the stalwart little crafts, poised in their cradles on the lapping edge of Lake Tanganyika, had their most challenging work still ahead of them.

The Battle for Lake Tanganyika

"His Majesty The King desires to express his appreciation of the wonderful work carried out by his most remote expedition." – Admiralty Telegraph

Sometime in the mid-1960s, Doctor Hanschell, as an elderly man, shared his reminiscences with British author Peter Shankland, and these were converted into a detailed history of the expedition entitled *The Phantom Flotilla*. Hanschell also tended to spare Spicer-Simson unnecessary criticism, but he admitted that the Commander was a generally self-serving and unprincipled fool. He took modest credit himself for shepherding Spicer-Simson past numerous potential disasters, but he was also prepared to concede that, under the circumstances, Spicer-Simson's methods worked surprisingly well. No deaths or injuries, no damage to property, and no unrecoverable losses had been recorded, and by any standards, that was a remarkable achievement.

In the meantime, the wider strategic position in East Africa had shifted somewhat in the months that the expedition had been en route. It was now December 1915, the Allied forces had been repulsed in an attempted amphibious landing in the territory, and German land forces still remained in control of the various frontiers. However, a Royal Navy blockade of the German East African coast was in effect, and the Allied forces were building forces to effect northern and southern invasions. A shift in naval power on Lake Tanganyika would entirely encircle the German garrison, which meant the expedition had arrived at precisely the right moment. As Frank Magee put it, "[I]t was to be our job to destroy the German fleet and thus assist in making effective the activities of the land forces operating against the enemy on their own coast." And as Hanschell was also quick to observe, for all of his past misfortunes, Spicer-Simson's luck during this adventure had been uncanny. Not a drop of rain had fallen when it would have stalled the expedition in its tracks, and yet, almost at the moment he set foot on the shore of Lake Tanganyika, a storm broke and rain fell. To the Europeans on the expedition, this was simply good luck, and it was welcome, but to the Africans, it was supernatural. To them, the aura that had surrounded Spicer-Simson as he led the caravan north was confirmed. As news of it circulated back down the route of the expedition, many a sage elder would have nodded his head in belief that a god had passed briefly through their lives.

The question now was whether his luck would hold. The *Mimi* arrived first, pulling into the Albertville rail siding on December 22, 1915. That night, she was unloaded and set in dry dock, and the following morning, *Toutou* arrived to be placed alongside her. As the engineers set to work preparing the two boats for launch, and as the gunner assembled and mounted their arms, Spicer-Simson sought out the necessary Belgian administrative officials and port authorities and began the uneasy liaison that would continue for the next few months.

The next day, as the crew paraded, Commander Spicer-Simson appeared wearing what looked like a khaki kilt. It was, he explained, a skirt, made for him by his wife, which was the only thing for the tropics, and this he intended to prove and would petition for its adoption as standard Royal Navy issue. It was suggested that it was not, in fact, a skirt, but a kilt. Undeterred, the Commander insisted that it was a skirt, and it remained thus.

He read a telegram received from the Admiralty that morning congratulating him on successfully executing his commission, and by evening, the flag of a Royal Navy Admiral was flying outside the Nissan Hut that the Belgian port authorities had made available for his use. In the meantime, it was vital to get the two boats in the water as quickly as possible. No one knew how accurate German intelligence was, and if they knew anything at all, a hostile visit from the Imperial German Navy might be expected at any time.

Work began immediately to build safe harbors for each of the boats and a launch ramp to get them in the water. The Belgians, to whom Spicer-Simson was now "á la Jupe", or "the Skirt", offered labor and facilitation, but in general, they stood back and observed, commenting among themselves but remaining aloof. On the evening of December 23, the two boats were launched, and the following morning, the engines were tested and the boats were drilled a few hundred yards offshore.

Meanwhile, on the eastern horizon, a white plume indicated German activity. Remaining just outside the range of the shore battery, the SMS *Kingani* watched with interest the activity underway on the Belgian side. By Christmas Day of 1915, after one full day on the water, leaks had been repaired and guns assembled. On the bow were mounted the 3-pound Hotchkiss navy guns and the Maxims afts. Riding the gentle swell of the lake, their lines were elegant and clean. Painted navy gray, they blended well, and their menacing little guns gleamed under a dousing of gun oil.

Like the Germans, the local Baholo-holo people were also beginning to take note of a major force in their midst. Rumors of the arrival of this great person attracted visitors from miles around, and the roar of the twin gasoline engines powering the *Mimi* and *Toutou* was of different stuff to the sedate "tuk-tuk" of the steamer, and both launches were evidently very well armed.

The Vice-Admiral, as he now styled himself, displayed his hubris and his bombastic self-confidence to the full. It impressed his audience deeply when he stood on a promontory and sent an illiterate semaphore message to the perplexed helmsman of the *Mimi* across a half-a-mile or so of water. He was apt to take his morning bath in public, where his full-body tattoos, draped across an ageing but still heroic frame, inspired awe. Some began to openly to venerate him as a god. Soon a concerned Belgian Jesuit missionary reported to Doctor Hanschell that strange fetishes resembling the Commander had begun to appear in the neighborhood, with his binoculars, the sceptre of his divinity, always represented.

News of all of this, of course, was quickly transferred across the lake, and at last the Germans began to realize that what they had been hearing in the weeks and month prior was true. Early on the morning of December 26, the SMS *Kingani* was again sighted patrolling offshore. The two little gunboats, tethered in the harbor like terriers and riding the swell back and forth, were ready. A message was delivered to Spicer–Simson, and with absolute self-possession, he conducted the usual Sunday parade and church service before ordering Chief Petty Officer Waterhouse to dismiss the divisions and to man the launches for immediate action.

As crews sped down towards the harbor, as shore details and the ship's crew slipped into their roles, and as the surrounding hills and bluffs rapidly filled with cheering native spectators, Spicer-Simson stepped out of his hut. Wearing his pressed skirt and smoking a monogrammed cigarette from a long jade holder, he was perfectly calm, perhaps even a little casual. His was the part of the tarnished Son-of-England, rising to claim his laurels. Even Doctor Hanschell was struck by the heroism of the moment. It was the stuff of imperial poetry, a Kipling-esque nod to the greatest empire known to man.

The two engines were fired, and they throbbed malevolently, waiting as the SMS *Kingani* crept closer inshore. She was wary of the shore battery, but she was close enough that her skipper, Captain Junge, could clearly be seen, his binoculars sweeping an innocuous shoreline. Spicer-Simson wanted to get one boat behind her, to put a wedge between her and her home port. As he watched through his own binoculars, however, it occurred to him that the *Kingani*'s forward gun was fixed and could only fire forward, so he ordered that the *Toutou* attack her port quarter and the *Mimi* her starboard, taking care at all times to remain to the rear. In this way, the *Kingani* would be at the mercy of the speed and maneuverability of the two launches. Spicer-Simson captained the *Mimi*, intending to lead the charge, with Lieutenant Waterhouse manning the forward gun.

At precisely 10:15, by prearrangement, a Belgian tug was launched and steered in the direction of the advancing *Kingani*, shielding from view the *Mimi* and *Toutou* as they edged out of hiding. A minute or two later, at a signal from the Commander, they roared into life, setting off across the water at a stiff 13 knots to intercept the unsuspecting steamer. The two launches quickly overtook the Belgian tug, riding a high wake and pushing aggressively forward over the swell, at which point they were revealed to the astonished observers on the deck of the *Kingani*. Captain Junge, momentarily confused at the sudden appearance of these two fast-moving little crafts, did not appear immediately to comprehend what was taking place. The SMS *Kingani* continued resolutely, bearing forward until it abruptly dawned on Junge that he was under attack. He ordered the *Kingani* into an immediate 90-degree lurch to port, screaming at the fire crew to stoke the boiler furnace.

It was hopeless, however, and he knew it. Shells were bursting in the water around the small steamer, and with a forward-facing gun, he was completely at the mercy of the enemy. Then, suddenly, an explosion erupted on the foredeck of the *Kingani* precisely where he was standing, and a cheer went up all along the shore. Captain Junge was killed immediately, and the brief but dramatic engagement was at an end. The stricken *Kingani* steered out of control for a few minutes before she came to a stop and raised the white flag. The action cost the lives of Captain Junge and two German Petty Officers, with the remaining crew captured.

When Doctor Hanschell encountered Spicer-Simson in the immediate aftermath of the battle, he found him in a state of disbelieving reverie, perhaps struggling to comprehend that a lifetime of bad luck, ignominy, and perceived incompetence had finally been put behind him. As a Royal Navy Commander, he stood poised on the very cusp of the recognition that for so long he had craved. It must certainly have been a moment of life-changing note for Spicer-Simson. A little quiet, inner reflection was quite appropriate at that moment, and the Doctor was very pleased to observe it.

And then, in classic form, the triumphant skipper ruined it all. As the excited discussion among the men dissecting the battle reached him, he could do nothing but brag. As the gunner of the RMS *Mimi*, Lieutenant Waterhouse claimed the killing shot, which Spicer-Simson acknowledged, but then added that with an exceptional gunnery officer such as himself directing fire, it was hardly surprising. "If only he could hold his tongue!" Doctor Hanschell thought bitterly, but Commander Spicer-Simson never could. He then went on to describe in detail his past successes as a gunnery officer, and as one by one his officers excused themselves, he found himself, in the end, addressing no one other than the dead Captain Junge. Pausing, he looked down at his slain rival, and bending over, he slipped a ring off the dead man's finger and put it on his own.

The SMS *Kingani*, meanwhile, was returned to the Belgian harbor base, where she was beached and repaired. Shortly afterwards, she was re-commissioned into the service of His Royal Majesty and renamed the *Fifi*. The Admiralty, when informed, forwarded its congratulations, and Spicer-Simson was promoted on the spot from Lieutenant Commander to full Commander, with seniority from the date of the action. This was a great relief to him, discharging him of the unenviable record as the oldest Lieutenant Commander in the Royal Navy. Commander Spicer-Simson now unquestionably outranked any local Belgian official, and rather than risk any possible friction, the Belgians officially handed over command of their flotilla, such as it was, to Spicer-Simson, which must also have been of great satisfaction to him.

The *Fifi*

The battle, however, was not over. There was work yet to be done, and furthermore, *Mimi* and *Toutou* had not survived their first action entirely unharmed. The 3-pound guns had damaged their mountings, and *Toutou* had accidentally rammed the side of the *Kingani*. Repairs were begun immediately. The *Fifi* was overhauled and made ready for action, and as all of this was underway, a constant vigil of interested villagers crowded the hill above the port, scouring the horizon for the inevitable appearance of the SMS *Hedwig von Wissmann*.

As daylight broke on February 9, 1916, over a month since the sinking of the SMS *Kingani*, a second plume of white smoke, at last, appeared on the east horizon, and the game was on once again. The Allied flotilla, minus the *Toutou*, which was still under repair, sailed forth to do battle. The Captain of the SMS *Hedwig von Wissmann*, initially suspecting that these pursuing crafts were Belgian and not to be taken seriously, continued his advance. At the moment that he was able to discern the white ensign of the Royal Navy, however, he realized, as had Captain Junge before him, that he was in deep trouble.

The *Hedwig* immediately turned and attempted an escape by pouring oil on the fires. *Mimi*, however, opened fire at about 3,800 yards, scoring several hits in the first few minutes of the battle. Behind *Mimi*, *Fifi*, now colored British and better armed than she had been under the German flag, opened up at 7,500 yards but was unable to register a hit. Closing the range to 5,600 yards, she was more successful, scoring approximately 40 hits out of 60 live rounds fired. A high-explosive shell penetrated the engine room, killing a native stoker and destroying the boiler. A second followed, causing similar damage to the engine. A third blew a substantial hole in the side of the ship, setting fire to the oil that was by then awash on the engine room floor.

In no time, the SMS *Hedwig von Wissmann* was engulfed in flames and billowing plumes of dark black smoke. The German Commander, Lieutenant Odebrecht, realizing that the ship was sinking, gave orders for it to be abandoned. Of the three wooden tenders attached to the ship, two were launched but were quickly hit, killing a German Warrant Officer and wounding several other crew members. The remainder took to the water. 8 black and 12 white crew members were later rescued from the water as the *Hedwig* slipped, hissing and billowing, beneath the calm waters of the lake.

The following day, the SMS *Graf von Götzen* appeared off shore, steaming slowly past the British base in search of the missing *Hedwig*. The expectation on the Allied shore was, with the startling success of the flotilla so far, that pursuit would be immediate and similarly successful.

Commander Spicer-Simson, however, appeared to experience a sudden crisis of confidence. He believed, or at least he professed to believe, that the Graf *von* Götzen was too much for his tiny flotilla, so no attack was ordered. According to the Doctor, the Commander seemed to palpably wilt and appeared suddenly to lose interest. He took to his bed for several days and would not be disturbed. From time to time, he would conduct a reconnaissance, ostensibly searching for the *Graf von Götzen*, but Doctor Hanschell was beginning to suspect that Spicer-Simson was avoiding action, wary of compromising the success that he had already achieved. A failure would have tarnished his heroism, and more than anything else, he wanted to return to London with that intact.

Conclusion

"First gain the victory and then make the best use of it you can." – Admiral Horatio Nelson

Thanks to action elsewhere, by the time Spicer-Simpson lost his nerve, it actually hardly mattered. The Allied offensive had began, and the Germans were on the run. The British tried several times to bomb her, but in the end, the SMS *Graf* von *Götzen* was scuttled in a harbor before she could fall into Allied hands.

The Allied forces, meanwhile, were soon besieging a handful of German settlements on the lakeshore, one of which was the town of Bismarkburg in modern Kasanga. There, a German garrison was surrounded by British forces and was likely to attempt an escape by water. On June 5, 1916, Spicer-Simson was ordered to approach the fort, seal off lake access, and destroy a small fleet of dhows anchored nearby. The support flotilla included *Mimi* and *Toutou*, but upon arriving a few miles offshore of Bismarkburg, Spicer-Simson was off-put by the sight of a battery of heavy guns lining the shore. To the dismay of his officers, he refused to go any closer and ordered a withdrawal. These were actually dummy guns, although in fairness, the Commander could not have known this. Nonetheless, it was all curious behavior, and before long, Spicer-Simson's command of the fleet had practically devolved to his junior officers, while he retired to his bed and could hardly be roused. Doctor Hanschell began to suspect that he was suffering from a mental breakdown and recommended a medical discharge, which Spicer-Simson agreed to with enthusiasm. He was generally judged to be guilty of dereliction of duty, and most analysis tends to agree that even if he had chased and lost the SMS *Graf* von *Götzen* in an open contest, and even if he had lost one of his own ships in pursuit, his reputation would not have been so damaged as it was by a perception of timidity or perhaps even cowardice. Doctor Hanschell could hardly equate the forthright and triumphant figure who had stepped off the *Fifi* after sinking the *Hedwig* with this tremoring wreck of a man barely able to walk. He wished him farewell from the quay at Bismarkburg, which was now in British hands, and watched him depart the theater with an air of tragedy, wondering what the future would hold for him.

Doctor Hanschell, in the meantime, stayed behind for a few months as the last actions of what has since come to be known as the Battle for Lake Tanganyika were fought. In a final ship-to-shore operation, Doctor Hanschell was wounded, taking a shard of shrapnel in the shoulder. He reflected afterwards that no injuries or deaths had been recorded thus far, and yet, at the moment that Spicer-Simson left the field, the first casualty was recorded. The injury was soon infected, and the Doctor contracted malaria, which left him hovering near death in a military hospital in Northern Rhodesia for several weeks. He finally made his way back to London a few months later. He naturally called on Spicer-Simson, who was back behind a desk at the Admiralty, and to his astonishment, he found the old, ebullient, self-satisfied character who he thought had perished somewhere on the shores of Lake Tanganyika.

In fact, Spicer-Simson had engineered his early departure with a clear sense of what an opportunity to get his story in first might mean. The first thing he did on his return to London was to apply for prize money for the acquisition of the *Kingani*, the capture of several dhows, and for blood money based on enemy casualties. A court ruled in his favor, based on a precedent established on the Great Lakes of North America during the War of 1812. He lectured and interviewed freely, and soon such press headlines were circulating as "Commander Spicer-Simson's Exploits on Lake Tanganyika" and "Nelson's Touch on African Lakes." Due to his efforts, it was now a matter of established history that it had been the *Graf von Götzen* that had declined battle, not he, and that he had fought and captured the Bismarkburg garrison almost single-handed. He was awarded a Distinguished Service Order, the Belgian Cross de Guerre, and the effusive congratulation of the Lords of the Admiralty, who now knew him by name. Doctor Hanschell was astonished, but not aggrieved, it would seem. In a way, Commander Spicer-Simson had earned these awards and accolades, and if he had to bend many conventions to win them, so be it.

Commander Spicer-Simson was never granted another command, but one can imagine that the most relieved at this was Spicer-Simson himself. The *Graf von Götzen* was re-floated after the war and restored for service as the MV *Liemba*. She still plies a route along the shores of Lake Tanganyika, operating as a ferry and supply ship, and is owned by Marine Services Company Limited of Tanzania. The *Fifi* was also repurposed after the war and turned to transport and ferry work, remaining in service, according to some accounts, until the 1960s.

The fates of *Mimi* and *Toutou* remain a mystery. *Mimi* is known to have remained in use as a gunboat for the remainder of the war, but besides that, nothing is known. Giles Foden, at the conclusion of his book, *Mimi and Toutou's Big Adventure*, notes the fact that in his search along the shore of Lake Tanganyika for the carcasses of either, he was told that *Toutou* had sunk near a village called Kabalangabo. He visited the place to investigate, and according to his account, he dived in briefly but saw no sign of a boat.

Ultimately, Commander Spicer-Simson found his way in due course to the office of Assistant Director of Naval Intelligence, with the rank of acting captain. Thanks to his fluency in French, he served as naval delegate and French translator at the Versailles Peace Conference in 1919. Later, after acting as secretary and official interpreter to the First International Hydrographic Conference, held in London in 1919, he was elected the first secretary-general of the International Hydrographic Bureau. In that role, he served from 1921-1937. In retirement, he and his wife moved to British Columbia, and there he gave occasional lectures on his command in Lake Tanganyika. He collaborated with Frank Magee in the composition of the famous *National Geographic* article, published in 1922, and he and Frank Magee remained friends. He died on January 29, 1947.

Online Resources

Other books about World War I by Charles River Editors

Other books about World War I on Amazon

Bibliography

Barrie, Alexander. *War Underground: The Tunnelers of the Great War.* London, United Kingdom: Privately published, 1962.

Barton, Peter, and Peter Doyle and Johan Vandeville. *Beneath Flanders Fields: The Tunnelers' War 1914-18.* Stroud, United Kingdom: The History Press, 2010.

Evans, Martin Marix. *Somme 1914–18: Lessons in War.* Stroud, United Kingdom: The History Press, 2010.

Freemantle, Michael. *Gas! Gas! Quick, Boys!: How Chemistry Changed the First World War.* Stroud, United Kingdom: The History Press, 2012.

Grieve, Captain W. Grant and Bernard Newman. *Tunnelers.* London, United Kingdom: Herbert Jenkins, 1936.

Haythornthwaite, Philip J. *The World War I Sourcebook.* London, United Kingdom: Arms and Armour Press, 1994.

Herwig, Holger H. *The First World War: Germany and Austria-Hungary 1914-1918.* London, United Kingdom: Arnold, 1997.

Jones, Simon. *Underground Warfare, 1914–1918.* Barnsley, Yorkshire, United Kingdom: Pen & Sword Books Ltd, 2010.

Thompson, Mark. *The White War: Life and Death on the Italian Front, 1915-1919.* New York City, New York: Basic Books, 2010.

Free Books by Charles River Editors

We have brand new titles available for free most days of the week. To see which of our titles are currently free, click on this link.

Discounted Books by Charles River Editors

We have titles at a discount price of just 99 cents everyday. To see which of our titles are currently 99 cents, click on this link.

Printed in Great Britain
by Amazon

17631140R00031